## Using the book

1 Begin by looking at the first story page (page 2). Look at the picture and ask questions about it. Then read the story text under the picture with your students. Use section 1 of the CD for this if possible.

2 Teach and check the understanding of any new vocabulary. Note that some of the words are in the **Picture Dictionary** at the back of the book.

3 Now look at the activities on the right-hand page. Show the example to the students and instruct them to complete the activities. This may be done individually, in pairs, or as a class.

4 Do the same for the remaining pages of the book.

5 Retell the whole story more quickly, reinforcing the new vocabulary. Sections 2 and 3 of the CD can help with this.

6 If possible, listen to the expanded story (section 4 of the CD). The students should follow in their books.

7 When the book is finished, use the **Picture Dictionary** to check that students understand and remember new vocabulary. Section 5 of the CD can help with this.

## Using the CD

The CD contains five sections.

1 The story told slowly, with pauses. Use this during the first reading. It may also be used for "Listen and repeat" activities at any point.

2 The story told at normal speed. This should be used once the students have read the book for the first time.

3 The story chanted. Students may want to chant along with the story.

4 The expanded story. The story is told in a longer version. This will help the students understand English when it is spoken faster, as they will now know the story and the vocabulary.

5 Vocabulary. Each word in the **Picture Dictionary** is spoken and then used in a simple sentence.

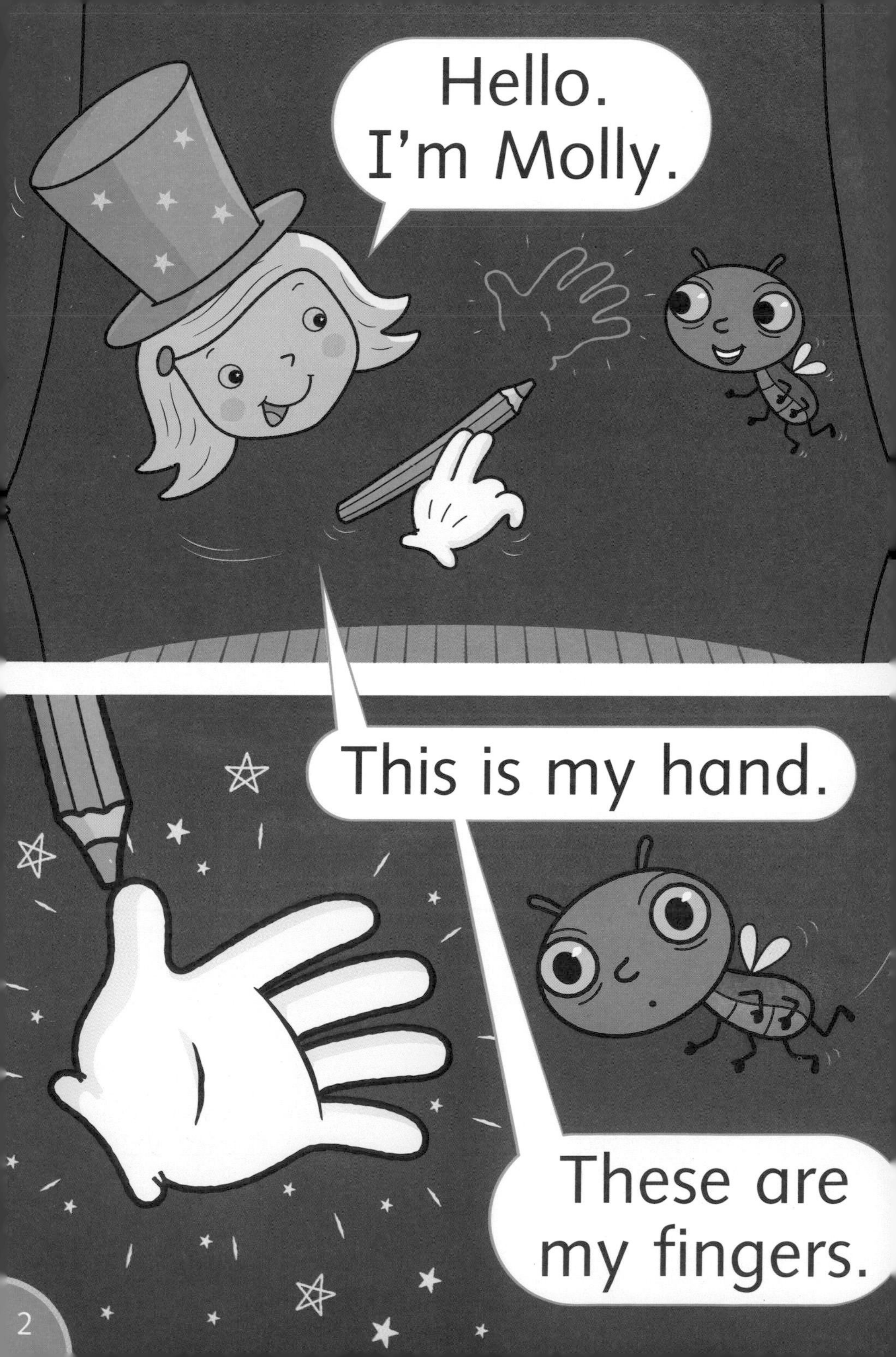
Hello.
I'm Molly.
This is my hand.
These are
my fingers.

# Meet Molly

Richard Northcott

Name _____

Age _____

Class _____

**OXFORD**
UNIVERSITY PRESS

# OXFORD
UNIVERSITY PRESS

Great Clarendon Street, Oxford OX2 6DP

Oxford University Press is a department of the University of Oxford.
It furthers the University's objective of excellence in research, scholarship,
and education by publishing worldwide in

Oxford New York

Auckland Cape Town Dar es Salaam Hong Kong Karachi
Kuala Lumpur Madrid Melbourne Mexico City Nairobi
New Delhi Shanghai Taipei Toronto

With offices in

Argentina Austria Brazil Chile Czech Republic France Greece
Guatemala Hungary Italy Japan Poland Portugal Singapore
South Korea Switzerland Thailand Turkey Ukraine Vietnam

OXFORD and OXFORD ENGLISH are registered trade marks of
Oxford University Press in the UK and in certain other countries

ISBN : 978 0 19 440087 9

Printed in Hong Kong

ACKNOWLEDGEMENTS
*Illustrations by*: Ian Cunliffe
*With thanks to Sally Spray for her contribution to this series*

# Trace and connect.

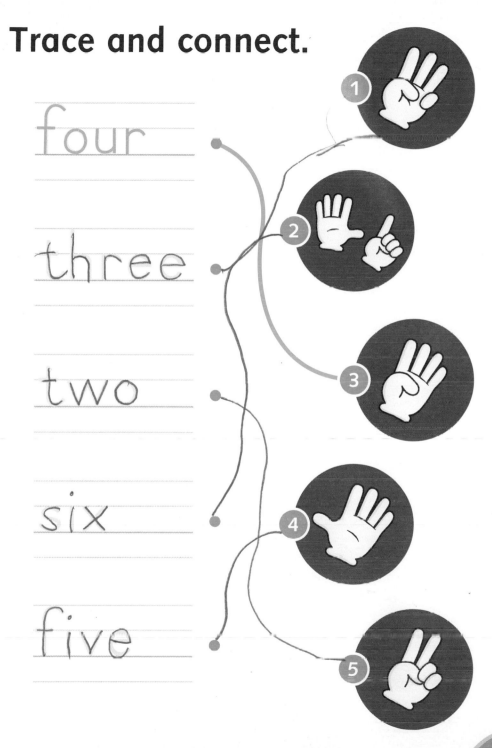

four

three

two

six

five

These are my legs.
One leg.
Two legs.

These are my feet.
One foot. Two feet.

# Circle `yes` or `no`.

1. It has one eye.   yes (no)
2. It has two eyes. (yes) no
3. It has one mouth. (yes) no
4. It has one foot.   yes (no)
5. It has eight feet.   yes (no)
6. It has six legs. (yes) no

This is Joe. He has blue eyes and a big smile. He is my friend.

# Circle.

**1** ~~These~~ (This) is a dog.

**2** (These) ~~This~~ are cats.

**3** (These) ~~This~~ are eyes.

**4** ~~These~~ (This) is my book.

**5** (These) ~~This~~ are my dolls.

**6** ~~These~~ (This) is my car.

7

# Trace and write.

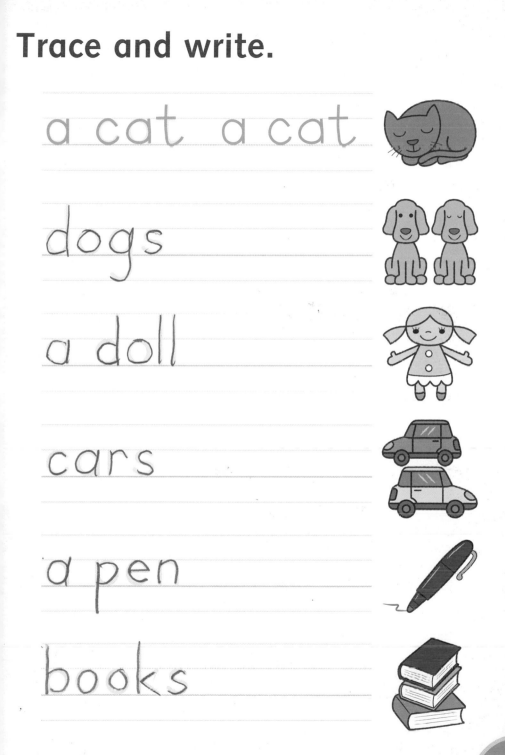

a cat   a cat

dogs

a doll

cars

a pen

books

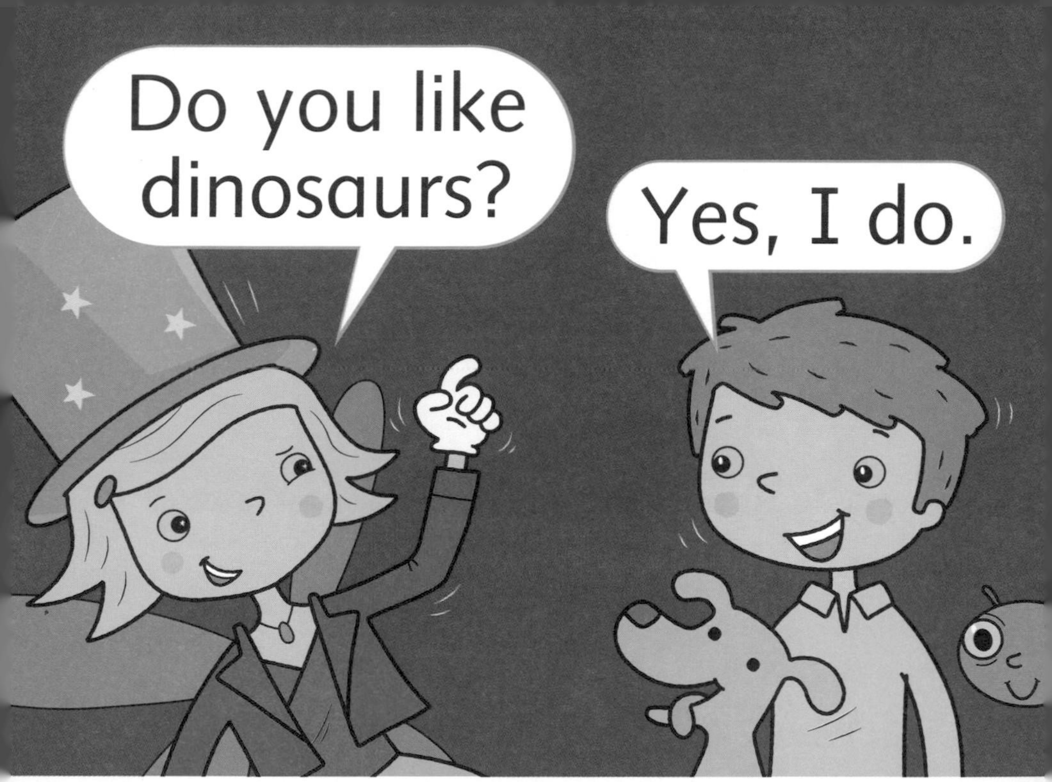
Do you like dinosaurs?
Yes, I do.

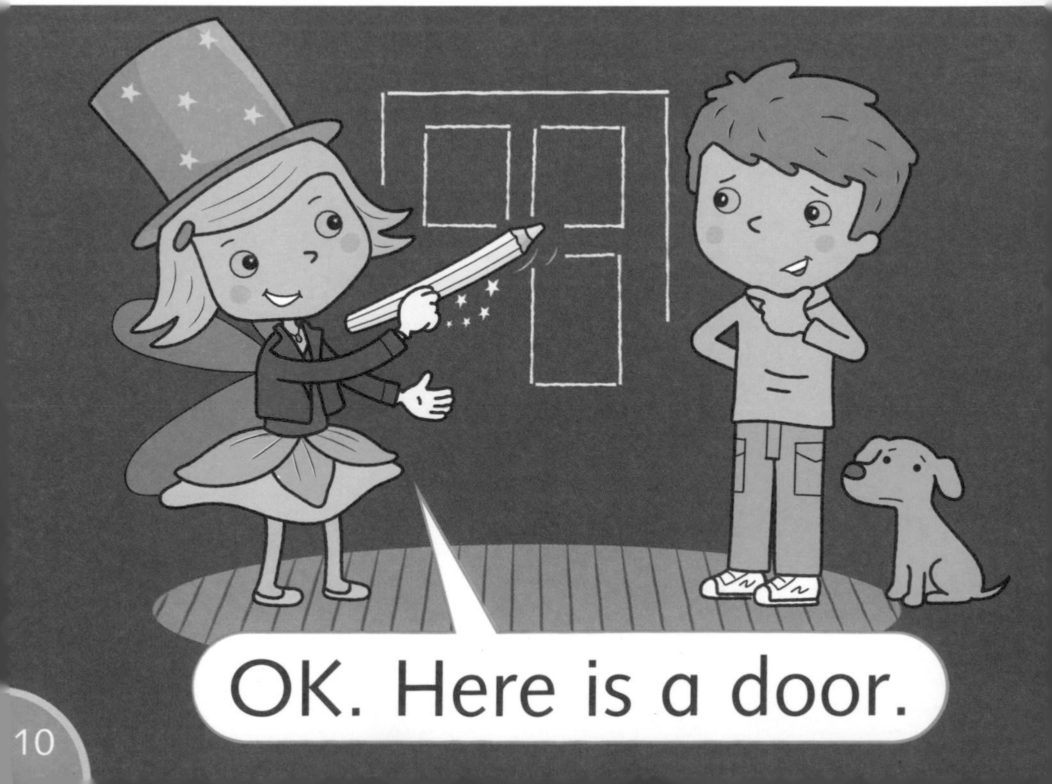
OK. Here is a door.

# Circle.

1. Joe likes ~~doors~~ (dinosaurs).

2. Joe has (green) blue pants.

3. Joe is a (boy) girl.

4. Joe has a green (blue) shirt.

5. Molly draws a (door) dinosaur.

6. Joe has black (white) shoes.

# Write the number.

① There is ⬚1⬚ green door.

② There are ⬚3⬚ houses.

③ There is ⬚1⬚ dog.

④ There are ⬚4⬚ cats.

⑤ There is ⬚1⬚ red car.

⑥ There are ⬚3⬚ trees.

You see. It's a dinosaur.

I like dinosaurs. Thank you Molly.
You're welcome.

# Circle yes or no.

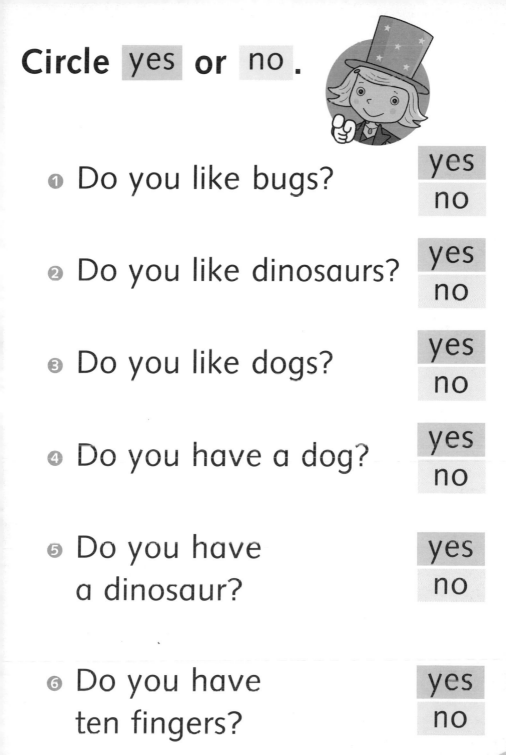

1. Do you like bugs?

   yes
   no

2. Do you like dinosaurs?

   yes
   no

3. Do you like dogs?

   yes
   no

4. Do you have a dog?

   yes
   no

5. Do you have a dinosaur?

   yes
   no

6. Do you have ten fingers?

   yes
   no

# Picture Dictionary

book

dinosaur

bug

dog

car

doll

cat

door

eye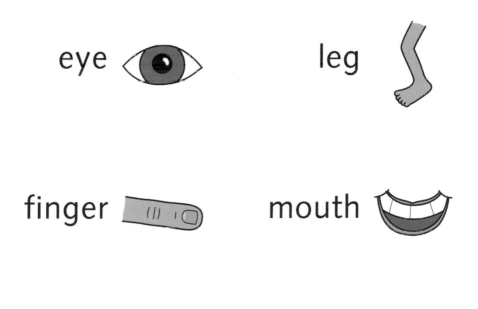

leg

finger

mouth

foot

pen

hand

tree

house

window

# Dolphin Readers

**Dolphin Readers** are available at five levels, from Starter to 4.

The Dolphins series covers four major themes:

## Grammar, Living Together, The World Around Us, Science and Nature.

For each theme, there are two titles at every level.

Activity Books are available for all Dolphins.

All Dolphins are available on audio CD.
(2 TITLES ON EACH CD 💿 SEE TABLE BELOW)

Teacher's Notes are available at **www.oup.com/elt/dolphins**

| | Grammar | Living Together | The World Around Us | Science and Nature |
|---|---|---|---|---|
| **Starter** | • Silly Squirrel<br>• Monkeying Around | • My Family<br>• A Day with Baby | • Doctor, Doctor<br>• Moving House | • A Game of Shapes<br>• Baby Animals |
| **Level 1** | • Meet Molly<br>• Where Is It? | • Little Helpers<br>• Jack the Hero | • On Safari<br>• Lost Kitten | • Number Magic<br>• How's the Weather? |
| **Level 2** | • Double Trouble<br>• Super Sam | • Candy for Breakfast<br>• Lost! | • A Visit to the City<br>• Matt's Mistake | • Numbers, Numbers Everywhere<br>• Circles and Squares |
| **Level 3** | • Students in Space<br>• What Did You Do Yesterday? | • New Girl in School<br>• Uncle Jerry's Great Idea | • Just Like Mine<br>• Wonderful Wild Animals | • Things That Fly<br>• Let's Go to the Rainforest |
| **Level 4** | • The Tough Task<br>• Yesterday, Today and Tomorrow | • We Won the Cup<br>• Up and Down | • Where People Live<br>• City Girl, Country Boy | • In the Ocean<br>• Go, Gorillas, Go |